The Power of Influence

By
John C. Maxwell

Honor Books
Tulsa, Oklahoma

The Power of Influence
ISBN 1-56292-967-4
Copyright © 2000 by John C. Maxwell
1530 Jamacha Road, Suite D
El Cajon, California 92019

Published by Honor Books
P.O. Box 55388
Tulsa, Oklahoma 74155

Introduction

Millionaire industrialist John D. Rockefeller once said that he was willing to pay more for this quality than for any other ability under the sun. President Theodore Roosevelt said it was the most important ingredient in the formula of success. That quality is our ability to deal with people—relationships. More than almost anything else in life, relationships make or break us.

That's why it's important to keep learning about them. This book is designed as a short course in relationships. May these timeless quotes and insights from men and women who understand people help you do the same.

John C. Maxwell

The Ten Commandments of Human Relations:

1. Speak to people.
2. Smile at people.
3. Call people by name.
4. Be friendly and helpful.
5. Be cordial.
6. Have a genuine interest in people.
7. Be generous with praise.
8. Be considerate of the feelings of others.
9. Be thoughtful of the opinions of others.
10. Be alert to give service.

If you're going to play together as a team, you've got to care for one another. You've got to love each other.

Vince Lombardi

The Law of Relationship says that every person is merely four people away from any other human on earth.

I don't know the key to success, but the key to failure is trying to please everybody.

Bill Cosby

No matter how much work you can do, no matter how engaging your personality may be, you will not advance far in business if you cannot work through others.

John Craig

You can't be any closer to God than you are
to the person you love least.

You can't make the other fellow feel important in
your presence if you secretly feel
that he is a nobody.

Les Giblin

It is very easy to forgive others their mistakes; it takes more grit and gumption to forgive them for having witnessed your own.

Jessamyn West

People aren't sales resistant—they are
salespeople resistant.

Mark Hebenstreit

Numbers don't mean anything . . .
because it's people that count.

Will Rogers

$$R + R - R = R + R$$

(Rules and Regulations minus Relationships equals
Resentment and Rebellion)

A drop of honey catches more flies
than a gallon of gall.

Abraham Lincoln

Friendship flourishes at the
fountain of forgiveness.

William A. Ward

If someone hurts you, first try to figure out whether that hurt was intentional or not. Not every hurt is an attack.

Getting people to like you is merely
the other side of liking them.

Ninety percent of the friction of daily life
is caused by the wrong tone of voice.

It is well to remember that the entire population of the universe with one trifling exception is composed of others.

J. A. Holmes

If you want to get along with people, pretend that you never knew whatever they tell you.

Each relationship nurtures a strength or a weakness within you.

Few things will pay you bigger dividends than the time and trouble you take to understand people. Almost nothing will add more to your stature as an executive and a person. Nothing will give you greater satisfaction or bring you more happiness.

Kienzle & Dare

Do to others as you would have them do to you.

Jesus (Luke 6:31 NIV)

A great man shows his greatness
by the way he treats little men.

Thomas Carlyle

If you want to lose friends quickly, start bragging about yourself; if you want to make and keep friends, start bragging about others.

> I will speak ill of no man and speak
> all the good I know of everybody.

Benjamin Franklin

> The true test of being comfortable with someone
> else is the ability to share silence.

Frank Tyger

The man who goes alone can start the day. But he who travels with another must wait until the other is ready.

Henry David Thoreau

Relationships are not formed but forged.

Anyone who loves his opinions more than he does
his brethren will defend his opinions
and destroy his brethren.

Let another man praise thee, and not thine own mouth; a stranger, and not thine own lips.

Proverbs 27:2

You cannot shake hands with a clenched fist.

Indira Gandhi

To handle yourself, use your head.
To handle others, use your heart.

John Maxwell

inety percent of the art of living consists of getting along with people you cannot stand.

Samuel Goldwyn

Instead of putting others in their place,
put yourself in their place.

Every man is entitled to be valued
by his best moments.

Ralph Waldo Emerson

Natural talent, intelligence, a wonderful education—none of these guarantees success. Something else is needed: the sensitivity to understand what other people want and the willingness to give it to them.

John Luther

One man working with you is worth
a dozen men working for you.

Herman M. Koelliker

People don't care how much you know
until they know how much you care.

John Maxwell

f you would win a man to your cause,
first convince him that you
are his sincere friend.

Abraham Lincoln

The most important single ingredient in the
formula of success is knowing how
to get along with people.

Theodore Roosevelt

I will pay more for the ability to deal with people
than for any other ability under the sun.

John D. Rockefeller

There is a rule in sailing that the more maneuverable ship should give way to the less maneuverable craft. I think this is sometimes a good rule to follow in human relationships as well.

Dr. Joyce Brothers

If you are suffering from a bad man's injustice, forgive him lest there be two bad men.

Augustine

Seek to be a plow rather than a bulldozer. The plow cultivates the soil, making it a good place for seed to grow. The bulldozer scrapes the earth and pushes every obstacle out of the way.

A Short Course in Human Relations . . .

The Six Most Important Words: "I admit I made a mistake."

The Five Most Important Words: "You did a good job."

The Four Most Important Words: "What is your opinion?"

The Three Most Important Words: "If you please."

The Two Most Important Words: "Thank You."

The Most Important Word: "We."

The Least Important Word: "I."

Don't use your people to build a great work;
use your work to build a great people.

Jack Hyles

There is no more noble occupation in the world
than to assist another human being—
to help someone succeed.

Alan Loy McGinnis

Practice the 101 percent principle: Find the one thing you agree on with another person, and then give it 100 percent of your encouragement.

John Maxwell

Assets make things possible.
People make things happen.

You can tell more about a person by what
he says about others than you can by
what others say about him.

It is one of the most beautiful compensations of this life that no man can sincerely try to help another without helping himself.

Ralph Waldo Emerson

In getting along with others, 98 percent depends on our behavior with others.

Marriage is the only union that can't be organized. Both sides think they're management.

Funny Funny World

I f you would have a happy life, remember
two things: In matters of principle,
stand like a rock; in matters of taste,
swim with the current.

Thomas Jefferson

We never know the love of our parents for us
till we have become parents.

Henry Ward Beecher

My most brilliant achievement was my ability to be
able to persuade my wife to marry me.

Winston Churchill

Two are better than one, because they have a good return for their work: If one falls down, his friend can help him up. But pity the man who falls and has no one to help him up!

Ecclesiastes 4:9-10 NIV

Even marriages made in heaven need
down-to-earth maintenance work.

Lloyd Byers

It is not marriage that fails, it is people that fail.
All that marriage does is to show people up.

Harry Emerson Fosdick

To keep the fire burning brightly, keep the two logs together, near enough to keep each other warm, and far enough apart—about a finger's breadth—for breathing room.
Good fire, good marriage—same rule.

Marnie Reed Crowell

God is the only third party in a marriage
that can make it work.

Faith makes all things possible.
Love makes all things easy.
Hope makes all things work.

Before a marriage, a man will lie awake all night thinking about something you said; after marriage, he'll fall asleep before you finish saying it.

Helen Rowland

The key to a perfect marriage
is not expecting perfection.

Marriage is an empty box.
It remains empty unless you put in
more than you take out.

Love at first sight is nothing special. It's when two people have been looking at each other for years that it becomes a miracle.

Sam Levinson

Courtship brings out the best.
Marriage brings out the rest.

Cullen Hightower

Love will find a way.
Indifference will find an excuse.

There are two great motivators in life. One is fear. The other is love. You can lead an organization by fear, but if you do, you will ensure that people won't perform up to their real capabilities.

Jan Carlson

We may not choose whom we will love
if we claim to be Christians.

A person needs to be loved the most when
he deserves to be loved the least.

The biggest disease today is not leprosy or tuberculosis, but rather the feeling of being unwanted, uncared for, and deserted by everybody.

Mother Teresa

Truth without love is brutality.
Love without truth is hypocrisy.

The love of our neighbor is the only door
out of the dungeon of self.

George MacDonald

Genuine love is a fragile flower. It must be maintained and protected if it is to survive. Love can perish . . . when there is no time for romantic activity . . . when a man and his wife forget how to talk to each other.

James Dobson

53

Faults are thick where love is thin.

The law of love always supercedes
the law of personal liberty.

You will find as you look back upon your life that the moments when you have really lived are the moments when you have done things in the spirit of love.

Henry Drummond

If you want to make your mother happy, talk to her. If you want to make your father happy, listen.

Human beings are the only creatures on earth that allow their children to come back home.

Bill Cosby

How far you go in life depends on your being tender with the young, compassionate with the aged, sympathetic with the striving, and tolerant of the weak and the strong. Because some day in life you will have been all of these.

George Washington Carver

A man should choose for his wife the woman he would choose as his best friend, were she a man.

There is no lonelier person than the one
who lives with a spouse with whom
he or she cannot communicate.

Margaret Mead

When I'm getting ready to reason with a man, I spend one-third of my time thinking about myself and what I am going to say and two-thirds thinking about him and what he is going to say.

Abraham Lincoln

People are lonely because they build
walls instead of bridges.

Joseph F. Newton

It's when you rub elbows with a man that
you find out what he has up his sleeve.

To keep your marriage brimming,
with love in the the loving cup,
when you're wrong, admit it.
When you're right, shut up.

Ogden Nash

Successful marriage is always a triangle:
a man, a woman, and God.

Cecil Myers

Train up a child in the way he should go
and walk there yourself once in a while.

Josh Billings

arents are prone to give their children everything except the one thing they need most. That is time.

Emma K. Hulburt

Never try to make your son or daughter
another you; one is enough!

Arnold Glasow

The best gift a father can give to his son
is the gift of himself—his time.

C. Neil Strait

The most important thing that parents can teach their children is how to get along without them.

Frank A. Clark

By the time we realize our parents
may have been right, we usually have children
who think we are wrong.

If there is anything better than
being loved, it's loving.

There is no more lovely, friendly, and charming relationship, communion, or company than a good marriage.

Martin Luther

God chooses our relatives; we choose our friends.

Never be yoked to one who refuses
the yoke of Christ.

The formula for achieving a successful relationship is simple: You should treat all disasters as if they were trivialities, but never treat a triviality as if it were a disaster.

Quentin Crisp

Most communication problems
can be solved with proximity.

Man and melons are hard to know.

Benjamin Franklin

A gossip is one who talks to you about others; a bore is one who talks to you about himself; and a brilliant conversationalist is one who talks to you about yourself.

Lisa Kirk

A person whose ship has come in usually finds
most of his relatives at the dock.

The harder you work at a relationship,
the harder it is to surrender.

The opinions which we hold of one another, our relationships with friends and kinsfolk, are in no sense permanent, save in appearance, but are as eternally fluid as the sea itself.

Marcel Proust

A man is known by the company he organizes.

Ambrose Bierce

A wise man associating with the vicious becomes an idiot; a dog traveling with good men becomes a rational being.

Arabic Proverb

You will acquire the vices and virtues of your closest associates. The fragrance of their lives will pervade your life.

John Maxwell

Tell me thy company, and I'll tell thee
what thou art.

Cervantes

Every man is like the company he is wont to keep.

Euripedes

n choosing a friend, go up a step.

Jewish Proverb

A wise man may look ridiculous
in the company of fools.

Thomas Fuller

He that lies down with dogs shall rise up with flies.

Latin Proverb

t is better to weep with wise men
than to laugh with fools.

Spanish Proverb

Familiarity breeds contempt—and children.

Mark Twain

Satan's friendship reaches to the prison door.

Turkish Proverb

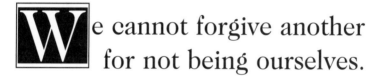

e cannot forgive another
for not being ourselves.

Ralph Waldo Emerson

None knows the weight of another's burden.

Thomas Fuller

Just as much as we see in others
we have in ourselves.

William Hazlitt

Most often it happens that one attributes to others only the feelings of which one is capable oneself.

Andre Gide

The longer we live, the more we find
we are like other persons.

Oliver Wendell Holmes

Hurting people hurt people.

John Maxwell

No man is much pleased with a companion who does not increase, in some respect, his fondness of himself.

Samuel Johnson

85

Love or perish.

One learns peoples through the heart,
not the eyes or the intellect.

Mark Twain

on't drown the man who taught you to swim. If you learned your trade or profession from the man, do not set up in opposition to him.

C. H. Spurgeon

It is a wise father that knows his own child.

Shakespeare

What the mother sings to the cradle
goes all the way down to the coffin.

Henry Ward Beecher

It is the atmosphere created primarily by the mother that makes a home worthwhile.

J. R. Bookhoff

A father is a banker provided by nature.

French Proverb

You don't have to deserve your mother's love.
You have to deserve your father's.
He's more particular.

Robert Frost

here parents do too much for their children, the children will not do much for themselves.

Elbert Hubbard

An angry father is most cruel toward himself.

Publius Syrus

Every beetle is a gazelle in the eyes of its mother.

Moorish Proverb

Romance fails us and so do friendships, but the relationship of parent and child, less noisy than all others, remains indelible and indestructible, the strongest relationship on earth.

Theodore Reik

There is scarcity of friendship, but not of friends.

Thomas Fuller

Acquaintance, *n.* A person whom we know
well enough to borrow from, but not
well enough to lend to.

Ambrose Bierce

A companion loves some agreeable qualities which a man may possess, but a friend loves the man himself.

James Boswell

It is by forgiving that one is forgiven.

Mother Teresa

A man should keep his friendship
in constant repair.

Samuel Johnson

orsake not an old friend, for a new one does not compare with him.

The Apocrypha

Between friends there is no need of justice.

Aristotle

Of all the things granted by wisdom, none is greater or better than friendship.

Pietro Aretino

Friendship is a strong habitual inclination in two persons to promote the good and happiness of one another.

Eustace Budgell

Wishing to be friends is quick work, but friendship
is a slow-ripening fruit.

Aristotle

Faithful are the wounds of a friend;
but the kisses of an enemy are deceitful.

Proverbs 27:6

The firmest friendships have been
formed in mutual adversity,
as iron is most strongly united
by the fiercest flame.

Charles Caleb Colton

True friendship is like sound health; the value
of it is seldom known until it be lost.

Charles Caleb Colton

Friendship makes prosperity more brilliant, and
lightens adversity by dividing and sharing it.

Cicero

The friendships which last are those wherein each friend respects the other's dignity to the point of not really wanting anything from him.

Cyril Connolly

The real friendships among men are so rare
that when they occur they are famous.

Clarence Day

It is one of the blessings of old friends that
you can afford to be stupid with them.

Ralph Waldo Emerson

eal friendship is shown in times of trouble; prosperity is full of friends.

Euripedes

The only way to have a friend is to be one.

Ralph Waldo Emerson

One loyal friend is worth ten thousand relatives.

Euripides

friend is a person with whom
I may be sincere. Before him,
I may think aloud.

Ralph Waldo Emerson

A good friend is my nearest relation.

Thomas Fuller

Friendship multiplies the good of life
and divides the evil.

Baltasar Gracian

friend may well be reckoned the masterpiece of nature.

Ralph Waldo Emerson

A sympathetic friend can be
quite as dear as a brother.

Homer

Your friend is a man who knows
all about you, and still likes you.

Elbert Hubbard

ove is rarer than genius itself,
and friendship is rarer still.

Charles Peguy

A true friend is the greatest of all blessings.

La Rochefoucauld

Hold a true friend with both your hands.

Nigerian Proverb

The proper office of a friend is to side with you when you are in the wrong. Nearly anybody will side with you when you are in the right.

Mark Twain

Friendship either finds or makes equals.

Publius Syrus

A man cannot be said to succeed in this life
who does not satisfy one friend.

Henry David Thoreau

ou cannot be friends upon any other terms than upon the terms of equality.

Woodrow Wilson

Whoso findeth a wife findeth a good thing.

Proverbs 18:22

Can two walk together, except they be agreed?

Amos 3:3

arriage is the perfection which love aimed at, ignorant of what it sought.

Ralph Waldo Emerson

A rare spoil for a man is the winning
of a good wife.

Euripides

Only a person who has faith in himself
is able to be faithful to others.

Erich Fromm

There is nothing nobler or more admirable than when two people who see eye to eye keep house as man and wife, confounding their enemies and delighting their friends.

Homer

A man's best fortune, or his worst, is his wife.

Thomas Fuller

The love we have in our youth is superficial
compared to the love that an old man
has for his old wife.

Will Durant (on his 90th birthday)

man should be taller, older, heavier, uglier, and hoarser than his wife.

Edgar Watson Howe

Man's best asset is a sympathetic wife.

Euripides

An ideal wife is any woman
who has an ideal husband.

Booth Tarkington

There are six requisites in every happy marriage. The first is Faith and the remaining five are Confidence.

Elbert Hubbard

Every mother is like Moses.
She does not enter the promised land.
She prepares a world she will not see.

Pope Paul VI

Back of every achievement is a proud wife,
and a surprised mother-in-law.

Brooks Hays

No man knows what the wife of his bosom is until he has gone with her through the fiery trials of this world.

Washington Irving

There is more pleasure in loving
than in being beloved.

Thomas Fuller

We should measure affection, not like
youngsters by the ardor of our passion,
but by its strength and constancy.

Cicero

successful marriage requires falling in love many times, always with the same person.

Mignon McLaughlin

Give every man thine ear, but few thy voice.

Shakespeare

Most Americans don't, in any vital sense, get together; they only do things together.

Louis Kronberger

ever speak of yourself to others; make them talk about themselves instead: therein lies the whole art of pleasing. Everyone knows it and everyone forgets it.

Edmond and Jules de Goncourt

129

A single arrow is easily broken,
but not ten in a bundle.

Japanese Proverb

Behold, how good and how pleasant it is
for brethren to dwell together in unity!

Psalm 133:1

The holy passion of friendship is so
sweet and steady and loyal and
enduring in nature that it will
last through a whole lifetime,
if not asked to lend money.

Mark Twain

Whoso loves believes the impossible.

Elizabeth Barrett Browning

Many waters cannot quench love,
neither can the floods drown it.

Song of Solomon 8:7

Love means giving one's self to another person fully, not just physically. When two people really love each other, this helps them to stay alive and grow. One must really be loved to grow.

Nancy Reagan

Love is the true price of love.

George Herbert

The course of love never did run smooth.

Shakespeare

reater love hath no man than this,
that a man lay down his
life for his friends.

Jesus (John 15:13)

If you've never been hated by your child,
you've never been a parent.

Bette Davis

I have found the best way to give advice to your
children is to find out what they want
and then advise them to do it.

Harry S. Truman

I talk and talk and talk, and I haven't taught people in fifty years what my father taught by example in one week.

Mario Cuomo

The most important thing a father can do for his children is to love their mother.

Theodore M. Hesburgh

Every generation revolts against its fathers and makes friends with its grandfathers.

Lewis Mumford

Build me a son, O Lord, who will be strong enough to know when he is weak, and brave enough to face himself when he is afraid, one who will be proud and unbending in honest defeat, and humble and gentle in victory.

Prayer of Douglas MacArthur

Other things may change us,
but we start and end with family.

Anthony Brandt

You don't choose your family. They are
God's gift to you, as you are to them.

Desmond Tutu

In the next year or so, my signature will appear on $60 billion of United States currency. More important to me, however, is the signature that appears on my life— the strong, proud, assertive handwriting of a loving father and mother.

Katherine D. Ortega, U.S. Treasurer

We need a better family life to make us
better servants of the people.

Jimmy Carter

Spoil your husband, but don't spoil
your children—that's my philosophy.

Louise Sevier Giddings Currey
(1961 New York Post *Mother of the Year)*

President Johnson and I have a lot in common. We were both born in small towns . . . and we're both fortunate in the fact that we think we married above ourselves.

Richard M. Nixon

Success in marriage does not come
merely through finding the right mate,
but through being the right mate.

Barnett Brickner

Marriage is not just spiritual communion and
passionate embraces; marriage is also three meals a
day and remembering to carry out the trash.

Dr. Joyce Brothers

he family is one of nature's masterpieces.

George Santayana

Bringing up a family should be an adventure.

Milton R. Sapirstein

Our children are not going to be just
"our children"—they are going to be
other people's husbands and wives and
the parents of our grandchildren.

Mary S. Calderone

boy becomes an adult three years before his parents think he does, and about two years after he thinks he does.

Lewis B. Hershey

Parenthood remains the greatest single
preserve of the amateur.

Alvin Toffler

More than in any other human relationship,
overwhelmingly more, motherhood means being
instantly interruptible, responsive, responsible.

Tille Olsen

Friendship with oneself is all-important because without it one cannot be friends with anyone else in the world.

Eleanor Roosevelt

Once you get people laughing, they're listening
and you can tell them almost anything.

Herbert Gardner

A person reveals his character by nothing
so clearly as the joke he resents.

G. C. Lichtenberg

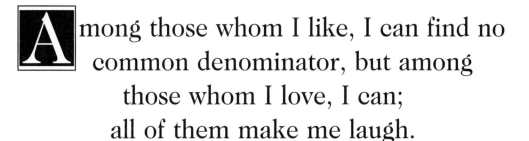

Among those whom I like, I can find no common denominator, but among those whom I love, I can; all of them make me laugh.

W. H. Auden

As iron sharpens iron,
so one man sharpens another.

Proverbs 27:17 NIV

If a man does not make new acquaintances
as he advances through life, he will soon
find himself left alone.

Samuel Johnson

hen the character of a man is not
clear to you, look at his friends.

Japanese Proverb

Be wiser than other people, if you can,
but do not tell them so.

Lord Chesterfield

Sometimes it's worse to win a fight than to lose.

Billie Holiday

friend can tell you things you don't want to tell yourself.

Frances Ward Weller

The richer your friends, the more they will cost you.

Elisabeth Marbury

If you want to grow up, go up. Associate with people whose achievements exceed your own and model the growth you desire.

John Maxwell

No man is an island entire of itself; every man is a part of the continent, a part of the main.

John Donne

John C. Maxwell, who has been described as America's expert on leadership, is founder of The INJOY Group, organizations dedicated to helping people maximize their personal and leadership potential.

Each year he speaks in person to more than twenty-five thousand people and influences the lives of more than one million individuals through seminars, books, and tapes. He is the author of more than twenty books with well over one million in print. A recent title, *The 21 Irrefutable Laws of Leadership,* appeared on the best-seller lists of the *New York Times,* the *Wall Street Journal, Business Week,* and the Christian Bookseller's Association.

Dr. Maxwell has two grown children and currently resides in Atlanta, Georgia with his wife of over twenty-five years, Margaret.

Additional copies of this book and other titles by John Maxwell are available
from your local bookstore.

Leadership 101

You Can't Be a Smart Cookie If You Have a Crummy Attitude

Honor Books
Tulsa, Oklahoma